Our Chore

We have a chore chart.
It tells us what to do.

Monday	
Tuesday	
Wednesday	
Thursday	
Friday	
Saturday	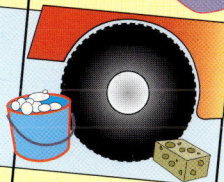
Sunday	

On Monday
we do the dishes.

On Tuesday
we take out the garbage.

On Wednesday
we sweep the floors.

On Thursday
we bring in the groceries.

On Friday
we sort the clothes.

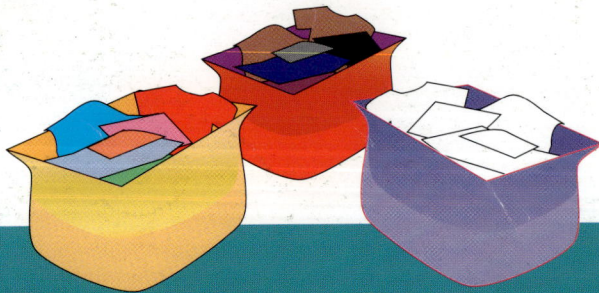

On Saturday
we wash the car.

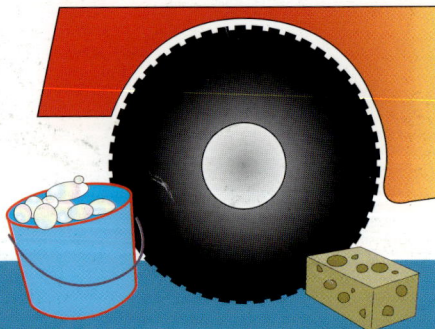

On Sunday – no chores!
We go to the park.